Akron-Summit County Public Library

PBZWR

D1525687

Take a trip to
IRAQ

Richard Tames

Franklin Watts

London   New York   Sydney   Toronto

Facts about Iraq

Area:
434,924 sq. km.
(167,925 sq. miles)

Population:
16,971,000

Capital:
Baghdad

Largest Cities:
Baghdad (3,236,000)
Basra (1,540,000)
Mosul (1,220,000)
Kirkuk (535,000)

Official language:
Arabic

Religion:
Islam

Main Exports:
Oil, dates, wool, hides,
cotton

Currency:
Dinar

Franklin Watts
12a Golden Square
London W1

Franklin Watts Inc.
387 Park Avenue South
New York, N.Y. 10016

ISBN: UK Edition 0 86 313 808 X
ISBN: US Edition 0–531–10651–9
Library of Congress Catalog Card No:
88-51322
© Franklin Watts Limited 1989

Typeset by Lineage, Watford
Printed in Hong Kong

Maps: Simon Roulestone
Design: Edward Kinsey

Stamps: Stanley Gibbons Limited
Photographs: Chris Fairclough 8;
Hutchison Library 3, 13; Christine Osborne
4, 6, 7, 10, 11, 12, 14, 15, 16, 18, 19, 20, 21,
22, 23, 25, 26, 27, 28, 29, 31; Jamie Simson
5, 24, 30; Frank Spooner 17

Front and Back Cover:
Christine Osborne

Iraq is an oil-rich Middle Eastern
country. Mesopotamia — a Greek word
meaning "the land between two rivers"
— is the old name for most of what is now
Iraq. It was the home of some of the world's
oldest civilizations. The name refers to
the area between the Euphrates and Tigris
Rivers, where most Iraqis now live.

The Tigris River rises in Turkey and flows through Mosul and Baghdad, the capital. At Al Qurnah it joins the Euphrates to form the navigable waterway called the Shatt al Arab, which flows into the Gulf. The Tigris is 1,850 km (1,150 miles) long.

The Euphrates also rises in Turkey and flows across the Syrian desert. It is 2,700 km (1,678 miles) long, the longest river in western Asia. It passes historic sites, such as Ur, Babylon and Nippur. Near the sea are marshes where people collect reeds.

The eastern part of Iraq is a highland zone, rising to 3,000m (about 9,840 ft) above sea level near the border with Iran. The mountainous northeast is the wettest part of Iraq, with about 40 to 60cm (16-24 inches) of rain in a year. Baghdad only gets 14cm (6 inches).

Western Iraq is an immense hot desert area known as the Hamad. Sand dunes cover large areas. There is little vegetation to support animals such as sheep and goats, so few people can make a living there.

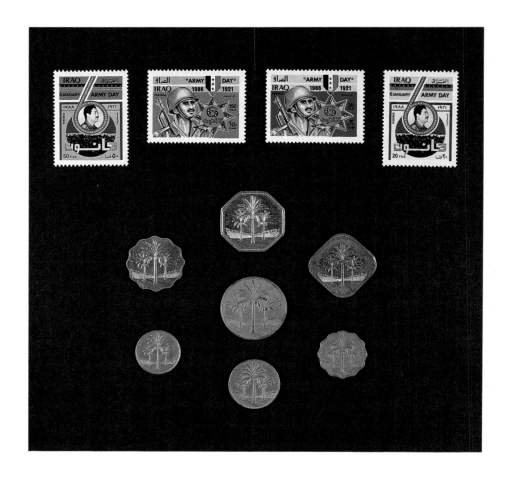

The picture shows some of the stamps and money used in Iraq. The main unit of currency is the dinar, which is divided into 1,000 fils.

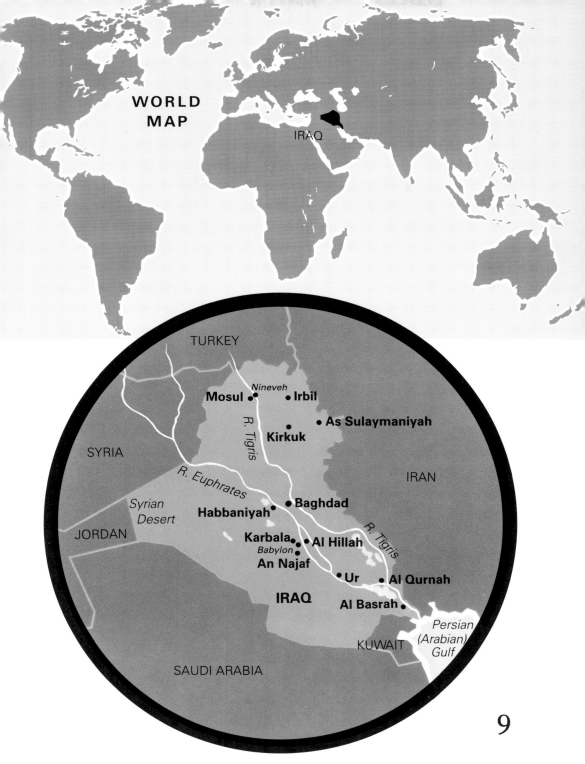

WORLD MAP

IRAQ

TURKEY

Mosul • *Nineveh* • Irbil

• As Sulaymaniyah

SYRIA

R. Tigris

Kirkuk •

R. Euphrates

IRAN

Syrian Desert

Habbaniyah • • Baghdad

JORDAN

Karbala • • Al Hillah

R. Tigris

Babylon

An Najaf

• Ur • Al Qurnah

IRAQ

Al Basrah •

Persian (Arabian) Gulf

KUWAIT

SAUDI ARABIA

9

Ur was the leading city in
Mesopotamia around 3000 BC. It's
famous ziggurat, or temple-tower, was
made of bricks. It was used for the
worship of a moon god, Nanna. Ur was
abandoned when the Euphrates changed
its course in about 400 BC.

10

Ur is mentioned in the book of *Genesis* as the home of Abraham. The site was rediscovered in 1854. Between 1922 and 1934, archaeologists excavated rich, royal burial grounds dating back to about 2500 BC.

The Arabs conquered Iraq in AD 637 and introduced their language and their religion, Islam. Today about three out of every four people are Arabs and 97 per cent are Muslims. This mosque, in Baghdad, was built in AD 1515.

Southern Iraq, where the Euphrates
and Tigris mingle together, is a marshy
region. Here some people live in houses
made of reeds, built on small islands of
mud. They travel around in small boats.

13

Iraq has several minority groups of people, including Iranians and Turks. The largest group, the Kurds, live in the mountainous northeast. They have their own language and culture and they would like to set up their own country, Kurdistan. These women are wearing Kurdish dress.

Only a few thousand Iraqis still follow the traditional Bedouin way of life as nomadic herdsmen, always on the move to find fresh pasture for their flocks. They roam the western desert, ignoring national boundaries and crossing into Syria and Jordan.

Badhdad has been the capital since Iraq became independent in 1927. It is a large modern city. Only one political party is allowed in Iraq. Its leader, Saddam Hussain, has been the President of Iraq since 1979.

In 1980, Iraq invaded Iran to get
control of the Shatt Al Arab waterway.
The fighting lasted until 1988 and cost a
million lives. Parts of big cities in both
countries were wrecked by long-range
missiles.

Basra is Iraq's second major city and the country's main port. Basra is near the border with Iran. It was badly damaged during the Iran-Iraq war and its port was put out of action. Another port, Um Qasr, near the border with Kuwait, was developed instead.

Seven out of every ten Iraqis live in towns or cities, though improvements in conditions are taking place in the villages. These improvements are paid for with money from oil sales. Here women are receiving clean water from a tanker. Many villages have recently got electric power for the first time.

Iraq's road system has also improved in recent years. These women are waiting for a bus. Many trucks and tankers drive through Iraq on their way from Europe and Turkey to the countries of the Gulf.

Oil accounts for nearly all of Iraq's exports and 98 per cent of the government's income. This tanker is leaving the oilfield near Kirkuk, Iraq's fourth largest city. Iraq has immense reserves of oil and the income from these should be able to pay for modern farming techniques and industries.

21

Farming employs 30 per cent of the work force. These people are harvesting wheat. Other crops include barley, rice, vegetables and fruits. Only 12 per cent of Iraq is farmland. Government experts are trying to improve irrigation and prevent soil erosion.

Most dates are grown around Basra in the warm, wet south of Iraq. Iraq is the world's largest producer of dates and accounts for four fifths of the world's trade in dates. Cotton is Iraq's other main cash crop. Hides and skins are also exported.

Sheep are valued for their wool as well as their meat and milk. Iraq has 8,500,000 sheep. The picture was taken at Al Qurnah, which legend says was the site of the Garden of Eden. The trees in the background are date palms.

Industry now employs more than a fifth of the workforce. These Kurdish children are weaving a carpet. Children are valued for their nimble fingers. Modern industries are being developed in Baghdad and Mosul. Some industries make chemicals from Iraq's oil.

A thousand years ago, when Baghdad was the capital of a great Arab empire, its merchants were famed for their wealth. Bazaars are now important not just for shopping, but also for meeting friends. Iraqis are enjoying a rising standard of living thanks to their oil industry.

Primary and secondary education in Iraq is free. The government regards education as a way of improving the standard of living. Iraq now has only 5 doctors for every 10,000 people, while nearby Kuwait has 13. But education now means there will be more doctors in future.

Iraq has six universities. These
students are at El Mustansiriyia in
Baghdad. Only about a quarter of the
adult population in Iraq can read and
write. Five daily newspapers are
published in the capital.

Most Iraqis enjoy a good diet. Eating meals together is important to family life. Everyone drinks fruit juice or milk. Muslims are forbidden by their religion to drink such things as wine or beer.

Throughout the 1970's Iraq's population was growing quickly and large numbers of young adults have moved from the countryside into cities. Villagers like these people in traditional dress form a smaller proportion of the population each year.

With the ending of the war against Iran in 1988, Iraq once again became free to use its great wealth for the benefit of its people. Iraq has also been generous in helping other Arab countries which are not lucky enough to have oil.

Index